A GIFT TO

FROM

WATCH OUT FOR OTHER GIFTBOOKS BY HELEN EXLEY

Wisdom for the New Millennium
Over 30s' Jokes
A Spread of Over 40s' Jokes

A Triumph of Over 50s' Jokes
Happy Birthday! (you poor old wreck)
Too Young for a Mid-Life Crisis

Published simultaneously in 2001 by Exley Publications Ltd in Great Britain and Exley Publications LLC in the USA.

12 11 10 9 8 7 6 5 4 3 2 1

Illustrations © Lincoln Exley Designs 2001
Selection and arrangement copyright © Helen Exley 2001
The moral right of the author has been asserted

ISBN 1-86187-120-1

Edited and words selected by Helen Exley
Illustrated by Sarah Jones
Printed in China

Exley Publications Ltd, 16 Chalk Hill, Watford, Herts, WD19 4BG, UK.
Exley Publications LLC, 232 Madison Avenue, Suite 1409, NY 10016, USA.
www.helenexleygiftbooks.com

ACKNOWLEDGEMENTS: The publishers are grateful for permission to reproduce copyright material. Whilst every reasonable effort has been made to trace copyright holders, the publisher would be pleased to hear from any not here acknowledged. *Pam Brown, Samantha David, Jenny de Vries, Pamela Dugdale, Marion Garretty, Stuart and Linda Macfarlane, Ingeborg Nelson, Maya V Patel, Pushpa Patel, Helen Thomson, Margot Thomson* published with permission, © Helen Exley 2001. All uncredited quotations are by *Stuart and Linda Macfarlane, Pam Brown, Carl Freeman* and *Joanna Jones* and are published with permission © Helen Exley 2001. A very special thank you to *Pam Brown* and *Stuart and Linda Macfarlane* for their invaluable contributions.

THE HAPPY BIRTHDAY BOOK

A HELEN EXLEY GIFTBOOK

NEW YORK • WATFORD, UK

YOU'RE THE ICING ON THE CAKE,

YOU'RE THE RIBBONS AND BOWS,

YOU'RE THE FIZZ IN THE

CHAMPAGNE,

YOU'RE SO VERY, VERY SPECIAL,

HAPPY BIRTHDAY.

HAPPY BIRTHDAY!

You're so special, so I hope that your birthday is special too!
I wish you brightly packaged gifts and greetings cards aplenty.
I wish you surprises and celebrations, and the warmth of your family around you.
I wish you joy today and always.

May this birthday, this year, bring you more joy than the last, more peace than the last, more beauty and more comfort.

More freedom from the mundane cares of everyday life and more time to experience sweet moments of calm.

YABODABADOOOOOOOOOO

DIARY OF THE WEEK:

MONDAY, DREAD — ARGH

TUESDAY, AWFUL — OOOOGH

WEDNESDAY, TERRIBLE — URGH

THURSDAY, HORRID — EEECK

FRIDAY, BIRTHDAY — YABODABADOOOOOOOOO

STUART AND LINDA MACFARLANE

MAY EACH DAY
COME TO YOU WRAPPED
IN TINSEL AND TIED UP
WITH RIBBONS.

MAY CHAMPAGNE MOMENTS
FILL YOUR LIFE.

MY WISH FOR YOU,
ON THIS SPECIAL DAY,
IS THAT LIFE'S PARTY
IS ALWAYS FILLED
WITH JOY AND LAUGHTER.

Today we wish you laughter
and song and silliness –
and people who love you
and people you love all about you,
sharing your happiness.

• • •

I wish you all you long for,
all you deserve. May this be
a birthday to remember with joy –
and the year ahead the best
you've ever known.

To an old wreck

It's your birthday – why not do something completely crazy! At your age could I suggest staying in bed might be wild enough.

STUART AND LINDA MACFARLANE

So many candles, so little cake!

AUTHOR UNKNOWN

Just think, if only you could snap your fingers on your birthday and never grow any older! HUH! Birthdays won't even let you do that because you've got that much arthritis your fingers won't snap.

SUSAN CURZON, AGE 12

Aaaaargh – goodbye youth.

STUART AND LINDA MACFARLANE

I wish that all your parcels turn out to be just what you wanted.

● ● ●

I would tear down a star and put it into a smart jewelry box if I could. I would seal up love in a long thin bottle so that you could sip it whenever it was needed if I could.

ANNE SEXTON (1928-1974)
IN A LETTER TO HER DAUGHTER

THIS IS YOUR DAY

This is Your Day. This is Your Time.
Dress it up in spangles.
Time enough ahead to be non-stop
sensible.

PAM BROWN, B.1928

There's always room for the
ridiculous – especially on birthdays.

PETER GRAY

It's all right to be happy on your birthday – there are 364 other days to be miserable.

LISETTE FAVIER

Your birthday is the one day in the year when you should forget all your worries and PARTY.

STUART AND LINDA MACFARLANE

PARTY! PARTY!

One cannot have too large a party.

JANE AUSTEN (1775-1817)

You know it's been a great party if:
- You're two years older when it ends.
- It makes front page news.
- Someone with a camera tries to blackmail you.
- People are still talking about it, ten years later.
- Riot police turn up – and decide to stay!

STUART AND LINDA MACFARLANE

LITTLE PIGGY DAY

Whether you are five or one hundred and five your birthday is the perfect excuse for over-indulgence.

STUART AND LINDA MACFARLANE

There's always room for ONE MORE.

PAM BROWN, B.1928

ALIVE!

The first fact about the celebration of a birthday is that it is a way of affirming defiantly, and even flamboyantly, that it is a good thing to be alive.

G.K. CHESTERTON (1874-1936)

KIDS' PARTY

A birthday cake must always have candles, and children dearly love the snapping cracker caps, and all the dainty favors which they take home. In fact the treasures that are taken home are half the party.

ELLYE HOWELL GLOVER

A CHILD'S SPECIAL DAY

A birthday lets you become a child again – enjoying cakes and balloons and opening gifts.

STUART AND LINDA
MACFARLANE

Most of us
can remember a time
when a birthday –
especially if it was one's own –
brightened the world
as if a second sun had risen.

ROBERT LYND

DOWN WITH BIRTHDAYS!

For all the advances in medicine, there is still no cure for the common birthday.

JOHN GLENN

JUST ANOTHER DAY?

ZZZZZZZ...

WAKENING...

A DAY OLDER...

BIRTHDAY!

A YEAR OLDER!!

CELEBRATE?

PANIC??

... BACK TO SLEEP

... DECISION DEFERRED

... ZZZZZZZ

STUART AND LINDA MACFARLANE

DISASTER
ON THE BIG DAY

*You know your birthday has been a
disaster when you are the only person to
turn up for your surprise birthday party.*

● ● ●

You know the fun has really gone out of
life when you forget your own birthday.

STUART AND LINDA MACFARLANE

OOOPS - I FORGOT!

For 364 days I remembered it was not your birthday. So don't be annoyed that for just one day I forgot that it was your birthday.

STUART AND LINDA MACFARLANE

Forget you're getting older,
Forget another year's gone by,
Forget it's your birthday,
I did!!!!

LISETTE FAVIER

I know some of your dreams.
To swim with dolphins.
To eat your way across Belgium.
To drowse on a beach of pure white sand
under whispering palm trees.
To ski in Canada.
To shop in Hong Kong.
To sail in a racing catamaran.
To give a home to sad, abandoned cats.
To ride the moors.

To have tea at the Ritz.
To travel to Venice on the Orient
Express.
May you do them all.

● ● ●

YOUR HEART'S DESIRES BE WITH YOU!

WILLIAM SHAKESPEARE (1564-1616)

Delights!

I wish you small delights – designer labels peering out from piles of tat at a sale, seeds that take and sprout and flourish, double yolks, a robin in the apple tree, coins in the gutter, a scary ride on a roller coaster, a small sticky kiss, a cat on a wall that needs its belly rubbed, a passing biplane flinging

itself into a loop-the-loop. A squirrel in your tree. An unexpected parcel. The train on time.

PAM BROWN, B.1928

I hope you find joy in the great things of life – but also in the little things. A flower, a song, a butterfly on your hand.

ELLEN LEVINE

WISHING YOU PEACE

MAY YOU BE HAPPY.
MAY YOU BE PEACEFUL.
MAY YOU BE FREE FROM SUFFERING.
AS I WANT TO BE HAPPY, PEACEFUL,
AND FREE FROM SUFFERING,
MAY YOU BE HAPPY, PEACEFUL,
AND FREE FROM SUFFERING.

A BUDDHIST METTALOVING
KINDNESS PRAYER

DEEP PEACE OF THE RUNNING WAVE TO YOU.

DEEP PEACE OF THE FLOWING AIR TO YOU.

DEEP PEACE OF THE QUIET EARTH TO YOU.

DEEP PEACE OF THE SHINING STARS TO YOU.

DEEP PEACE OF THE SON OF PEACE TO YOU.

GAELIC BLESSING

Have you ever thought that the candles on a birthday cake represent your accomplishments as well as years? The little things you've done... an encouraging word or a helping hand perhaps....

• • •

The great thing about getting older is that you don't lose all of the other ages you've been.

MADELINE L'ENGLE

We are always
the same age inside.

GERTRUDE STEIN

What can I say to you? I am perhaps the oldest musician in the world. I am an old man, but in many senses a very young man. And this is what I want you to be – young, young all your life, and to say things to the world that are true.

PABLO CASALS (1876-1973)

We turn not older with years, but newer every day.

EMILY DICKINSON
(1830-1886)

The older the fiddle, the sweeter the tune.

ENGLISH PROVERB

When somebody says to me – which they do like every five years – "How does it feel to be over the hill," my response is, "I'm just heading up the mountain."

JOAN BAEZ

LOOKING FORWARD

YOUR AGE DEPENDS ON THE ELASTICITY OF YOUR SPIRIT AND THE VIGOR OF YOUR MIND — AND ON HOW MANY BIRTHDAYS YOU'RE STILL LOOKING FORWARD TO.

EUGENE P. BERTIN

YOUTH IS HAPPY BECAUSE IT HAS THE ABILITY TO SEE BEAUTY. ANYONE WHO KEEPS THE ABILITY TO SEE BEAUTY NEVER GROWS OLD.

FRANZ KAFKA
(1883-1924)

FOLLOW YOUR DREAMS

May you always find new roads
to travel;
new horizons to explore;
new dreams to call your own.

MARK ORTMAN

I think that wherever your journey takes
you there are new gods waiting there,
with divine patience – and laughter.

SUSAN M. WATKINS, B.1945

IRISH TOASTS

May the best of this year be the worst of next.

And may the face of every good news and the back of every bad news be toward us in the coming year.

May you live to be a hundred years With one extra year to repent.

TODAY YOUR LIFE BEGINS...

It's never too late – never too late to start over, never too late to be happy.

JANE FONDA, B.1937

May you live all the days of your life.

JONATHAN SWIFT (1667-1745)

HAVE NO REGRETS

When I'm old I'm never going
to say, "I didn't do this" or,
"I regret that". I'm going to say,
"I don't regret a damn thing.
I came, I went, and I did it all."

KIM BASINGER

Today is the first day
of the rest of your life.

DALE CARNEGIE

I wish you a day filled with smiles and surprises, and a year of adventures and excitement.

I wish you discoveries and marvels. I wish you success. I wish you joy and peace and deep contentment. And always, always, love.

I wish you quiet sleep, good dreams, happy awakenings.

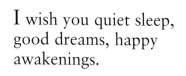

BE HAPPY IN YOUR OWN SPECIAL WAY.

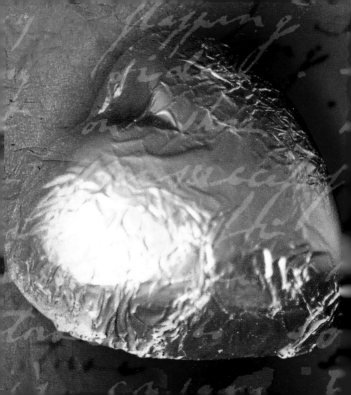